MEET GAGA!

There's no doubt that Lady Gaga has been the biggest pop sensation of the century. With her cutting edge fashion sense, her theatrical on- and off-stage persona, and her catchy tunes, Lady Gaga has risen from New York obscurity to become one of the most talked-about celebs out there! She's sold over ten million albums worldwide, sold more digital downloads than any other artist, and has had cameo appearances on hot shows like *Gossip Girl.* Amazing!

But her rise to the top hasn't been easy. She was dropped from a record label, had her heart broken, and had to face her demons – she faced knockbacks that would have made the average person turn around and run.

But instead of turning and running away, the sassy chick, who was born Stefani Joanne Angelina Germanotta, was just even more determined to get to the top. This is her incredible story, plus loads of secrets from her past!

GAGA ⚡ FACTFILE

BIRTH NAME **//** STEFANI JOANNE ANGELINA GERMANOTTA
NICKNAME **//** GAGA
DATE OF BIRTH **//** 28 MARCH 1986
STAR SIGN **//** ARIES
PLACE OF BIRTH **//** NEW YORK CITY, USA
HEIGHT **//** 5' 1"
TRADE MARKS **//** HAIR BOW, PLATINUM BLONDE HAIR,
WEARING WIGS AND HAIR PIECES, WEARING CRAZY OUTFITS
FAMILY **//** HER PARENTS ARE OF ITALIAN ORIGIN, AND
SHE HAS ONE YOUNGER SISTER
NATURAL HAIR COLOUR **//** BRUNETTE
FAVOURITE FOOD **//** ITALIAN FOOD LIKE MEATBALLS,
SPAGHETTI, PIZZA AND PASTA. SHE ALWAYS ASKS FOR
HUMMUS BACKSTAGE AT HER SHOWS. SHE LOVES GUMMY
WORMS TOO. YUM!
FAVOURITE ARTIST **//** ANDY WARHOL
FAVOURITE BOOK **//** *LETTERS TO A YOUNG POET* BY RAINER
MARIA RILKE
FAVOURITE SINGERS **//** DAVID BOWIE, MADONNA, CYNDI
LAUPER, BRITNEY SPEARS, GRACE JONES, MICHAEL JACKSON,
FREDDIE MERCURY
FAVOURITE BANDS **//** MÖTLEY CRÜE, THE KILLERS, LED
ZEPPELIN, 'N SYNC
FAVOURITE CITY **//** HER HOMETOWN, NEW YORK
FAVOURITE SONG **//** 'LET'S DANCE' BY DAVID BOWIE
FAVOURITE PERFUME **//** RALPH BY RALPH LAUREN
OR MARC JACOBS DAISY
FAVOURITE FILM **//** THE FRENCH FILM *LA HAINE*
FAVOURITE PAINTING **//** *NIGHTHAWKS* BY EDWARD HOPPER

A STAR IS BORN

Even as a young child, Stefani Germanotta showed a real talent for music. She started playing the piano at age four, and although she hated practising at first, her mum made her sit there for an hour a day – so eventually she started playing, and found that by practising for a couple of hours every day, she soon became really good.

BORN TO PERFORM

She was also a born performer, who loved to shock. 'I discovered my love of shock art at an early age,' she says. 'I always wanted to be a star. I always wanted to be some kind of commercial vehicle that had the attention of the world and could say and do things to inspire people. That's just always been what I wanted to do.'

Stefani's love of music and singing meant she was no stranger to performing pop songs for her family and friends. One day, she was wandering around a store in downtown New York, singing away to herself, not realising that anyone was listening. A guy who was working in the store came over and told her she had a great voice, and gave her the card of his uncle. His uncle just happened to be a famous voice coach called Don Lawrence, who coached Mariah Carey! Can you imagine?! Don managed to fit young Stefani into his busy schedule, and recognised her potential. He told her that as well as practising the piano, she should start writing songs too. She was barely into her teenage years but she followed his advice. She went straight home and started writing songs – and never stopped.

GAGA GOSSIP
Her stage name, Lady Gaga, is a reference to the song *Radio Ga Ga* by Queen. Her producer and friend Rob Fusari called her Gaga because she was so theatrical.

Lady Gaga's star sign is Aries, which means she loves her freedom and is really open to new ideas . . . sounds like Gaga! Ariens have the following positive character traits: courage, self-confidence, determination, enthusiasm, pioneering, adventurous, dynamic, energetic, quick-witted, open-hearted, creative, independent. The negative sides of Ariens means they can be impatient, intolerant, quick-tempered, impulsive, and selfish.

Love interests? Ariens are considered to be most compatible with those born under the Leo and Sagittarius signs.

WHAT STAR SIGN ARE YOU? LOOK AT THIS CHART AND SEE WHO YOU ARE MOST COMPATIBLE WITH!

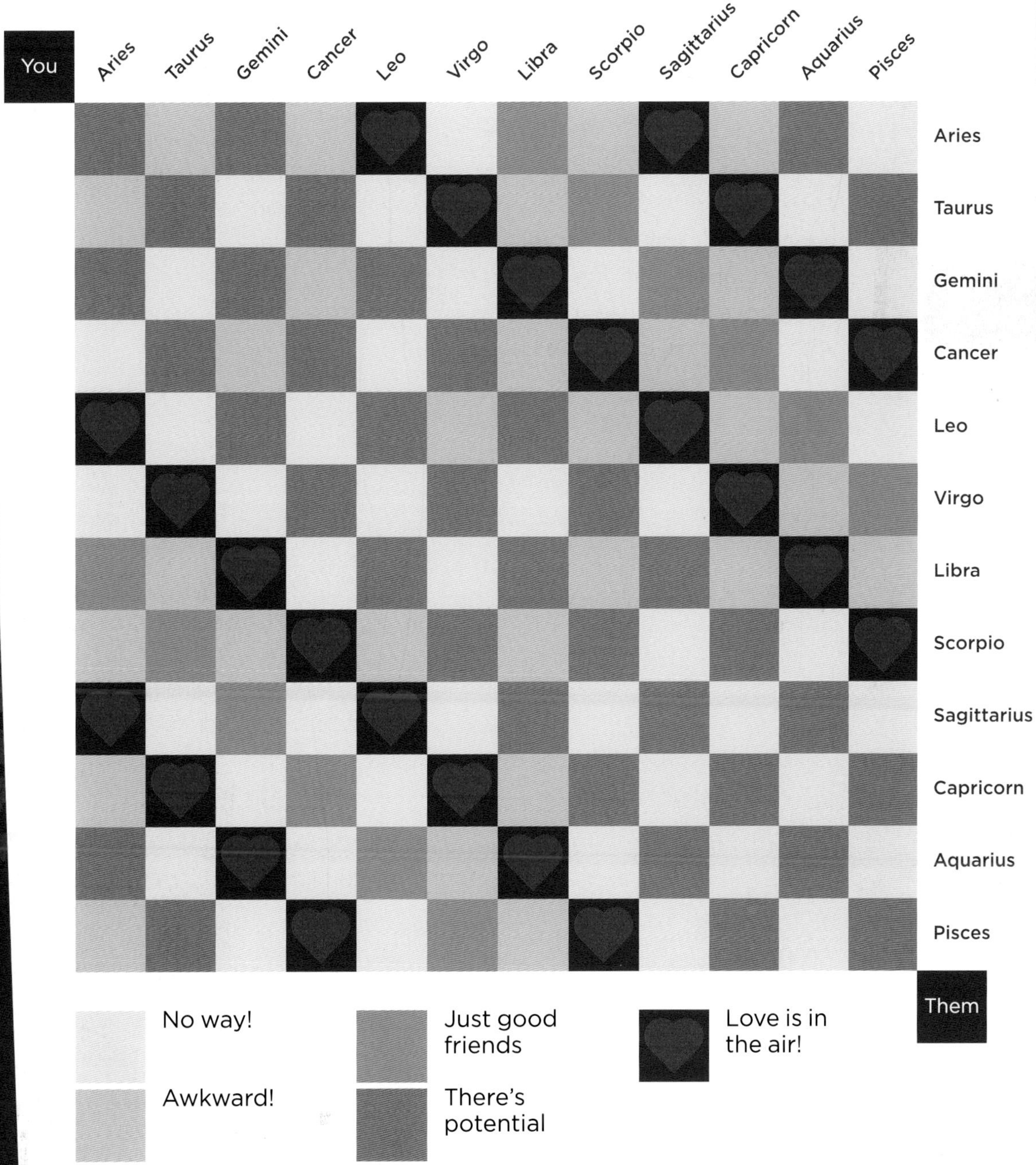

You

Aries · Taurus · Gemini · Cancer · Leo · Virgo · Libra · Scorpio · Sagittarius · Capricorn · Aquarius · Pisces

Aries
Taurus
Gemini
Cancer
Leo
Virgo
Libra
Scorpio
Sagittarius
Capricorn
Aquarius
Pisces

Them

No way!

Awkward!

Just good friends

There's potential

Love is in the air!

SCHOOL DAYS

Because her parents had been so successful in business, they decided to send Stefani and her sister to the private all-girl Catholic school, Convent of the Sacred Heart, in New York. The school was totally exclusive, and was where all the elite would send their daughters – the likes of Paris and Nicky Hilton to name just two!

Sacred Heart was a strict school, where all the girls were expected to study hard, and were taught to think of themselves as leaders of the future. The girls also had to wear a uniform. Stefani was a good student – she studied really hard and got top grades in all her classes. But she found the strict environment hard to deal with, and it was difficult to fit in with all the socialites and the girls from upper-class families. 'Paris and Nicky Hilton went to my school. They're very pretty, and very, very clean. It's impressive to be that perfect all the time. In commercial terms, they've been quite an influence on me.'

ARTS VS. BOYS:
THE ARTS ALL THE WAY!

The school's great arts programme meant that, alongside the usual things like literature and mathematics classes, young Stefani got to focus on studying piano, voice and drama – three things she was already mad about. She was more interested in art and music than she was in boys – something that a lot of girls at the school found pretty weird. She loved playing the piano and practised all the time, writing songs as well as perfecting her playing technique.

The school had fancy marble statues and sweeping staircases, like you'd expect to find on a film set or in a castle – a truly magical setting to go to school in. Stefani kept up her vocal coaching outside of school, and in school she joined every choir and singing group there was, and performed in musicals and shows that the school would put on.

SCHOOL TRIVIA
Favourite subjects at school – music, art, drama

UNIQUE STYLE ROCKS!

The popular girls at Stefani's school would tease her for her eccentric dress sense, so she was very much the arty girl who didn't fit in. She experimented with her look and style even as a young teen. 'I used to get in trouble a lot for wearing very low-cut shirts and see-through stuff with bras,' she says. 'I was actually a very good student. I just sort of stuck out like a sore thumb – no different than today.'

'I DIDN'T FIT IN AT HIGH SCHOOL AND I FELT LIKE A FREAK . . . SO I LIKE TO CREATE THIS ATMOSPHERE FOR MY FANS WHERE THEY FEEL LIKE THEY HAVE A FREAK IN ME TO HANG OUT WITH AND THEY DON'T FEEL ALONE.'

GAGA GOSSIP
'I was the arty girl, the theatre chick. I dressed differently and I came from a different social class from the other girls. I was more of an average schoolgirl.'

MAKING
IT

After Stefani finished high school, she found herself in a dilemma. She had been accepted into the Tisch School of the Arts at New York University a year early, but she had a niggling feeling at the back of her mind that it wasn't the right choice. She was studying musical theatre, and even though she loved all her classes, she felt like she was missing out on an opportunity outside of university.

She worked hard, but after half a year, she knew what she needed to do. She told her parents she was going to drop out to pursue a life of music in the real world.

Her parents couldn't believe it but they knew how determined their daughter was. Once she had decided to do something, it was impossible to change her mind. Her dad made a deal with her: she had a year to get signed by a record label otherwise she had to go back to university.

Stefani knew she could do it. So she dropped out of school and moved into an apartment on her own, working as a waitress to pay her own way, and writing music in her spare time.

She played gig after gig, and one night she was spotted at a talent show. Record producer Rob Fusari – who had written hits for Destiny's Child – came over to her after the show, and told her he wanted to write music with her. They worked together and wrote songs that would end up on her first album – songs like 'Beautiful, Dirty, Rich' and 'Paparazzi'. It was during this time that Rob nicknamed her Gaga – and the name stuck!

'I DID THIS THE WAY YOU ARE SUPPOSED TO. I PLAYED EVERY CLUB IN NEW YORK CITY AND I BOMBED IN EVERY CLUB AND THEN KILLED IT IN EVERY CLUB AND I FOUND MYSELF AS AN ARTIST. I LEARNED HOW TO SURVIVE AS AN ARTIST, GET REAL, AND HOW TO FAIL AND THEN FIGURE OUT WHO I WAS AS A SINGER AND A PERFORMER. I WORKED HARD.'

On the back of great reviews of her performances in New York, she managed to swing a record deal with New York label Def Jam. But it wasn't to be. Although they recognised her talent, the record label had trouble knowing how to market her. She refused to wear trousers and would turn up for meetings and to work in just a leotard and legwarmers – just like the Gaga we know and love today! After a few months, she was dropped from the label.

GAGA BOUNCES BACK

But Gaga refused to be defeated. She kept on writing music and playing gigs, and started go-go dancing in clubs with her close friend Lady Starlight. The word about her huge talent started to spread and she was introduced to another music producer, called RedOne. Together they wrote the infectious dance track 'Boys Boys Boys', and it was around this time she was signed as a songwriter to Interscope.

She started working on tracks for numerous artists, including one of her all time heroes, Britney Spears! But she kept working on her own tracks too, and before long, she had written an entire album's worth of amazing pop songs – as well as songs for artists like Britney and the Pussycat Dolls!

THE FAME

The Fame had been inspired by Gaga's time living in New York, trying to get a break in the music industry. 'It's about how anyone can feel famous,' she explains. 'Pop culture is art. It doesn't make you cool to hate pop culture, so I embraced it and you hear it all over *The Fame*. But, it's a sharable fame. I want to invite you all to the party. I want people to feel a part of this lifestyle.'

GLOBETROTTING GAGA!

Once the album was completed, Gaga set off on tour around America to promote it. She was writing songs for the New Kids On The Block album, and was chosen to be the opening act on their comeback tour. She was also lucky enough to land the opening slot on the Pussycat Dolls world tour, which took her out of America and as far from home as the UK and Australia.

BRIT-TASTIC!

The strong shows on her tour won her thousands of fans, and two number one singles in the infectious pop bullets 'Just Dance' and 'Poker Face'. People loved her off-the-wall videos so much they ended up all over the awards ceremonies – with 'Paparazzi' winning both Best Art Direction and Best Special Effects at the 2009 MTV Video Music Awards. 'Poker Face' won a Grammy Award for Best Dance Recording, and *The Fame* even won the Grammy Award for Best Electronic/Dance Album. Not satisfied with that, *The Fame* also won Best International Album at the 2010 BRIT Awards, and Gaga herself won Best International Breakthrough Artist and Best International Female. Amazing achievements!

DIAMONDS ARE A GIRL'S BEST FRIEND

Even though it took some time to take off in her home country of America, Gaga's debut album *The Fame* ended up going platinum in 18 countries and eventually went diamond worldwide, meaning that it had sold over 10 million copies around the world! A truly amazing feat for the street-smart girl from New York!

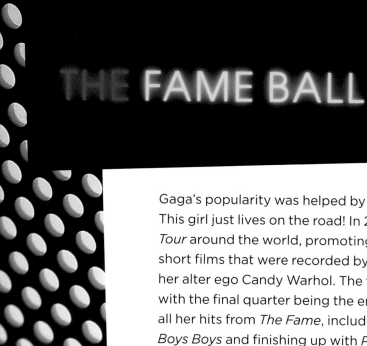

THE FAME BALL

Gaga's popularity was helped by her relentless touring schedule. This girl just lives on the road! In 2009, Gaga took her *Fame Ball Tour* around the world, promoting *The Fame*. The show featured short films that were recorded by Gaga, in which she appeared as her alter ego Candy Warhol. The films split the show into four parts, with the final quarter being the encore, and the set list including all her hits from *The Fame*, including *Paparazzi*, *LoveGame*, *Boys Boys Boys* and finishing up with *Poker Face*. The tour hit the USA, Canada, Russia, New Zealand, Australia, Singapore, UK, Germany, France, Japan, Israel and many more countries, and it was on this tour that Gaga debuted some of her most cutting edge looks – including her awesome bubble dress, which was classic Gaga!

'IN MY EARLIER DAYS OF WRITING FOR MYSELF, I WANTED SONGS TO BE MORE COMPLEX. I THOUGHT THEY HAD TO BE FOR ME TO BE TAKEN SERIOUSLY AS AN ARTIST. BUT WRITING FOR OTHER PEOPLE, YOU GET TO LEARN THINGS ABOUT YOURSELF AND TAKE ON THEIR INSECURITIES. NOW I CAN APPRECIATE AND INCORPORATE MORE SIMPLICITY IN LYRICS AND MELODY.'
Gaga on writing songs for other artists

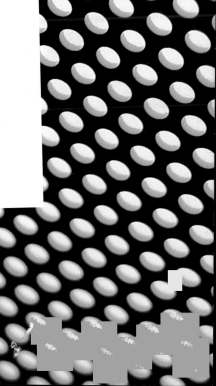

THE FAME MONSTER

Having spent so much time on the road definitely took its toll on Gaga. She played hundreds of dates in 2009, rushing from city to city, country to country, always working and sometimes only sleeping for a couple of hours per night.

And even though *The Fame* had been incredibly popular and she had managed to win so many awards, her punishing schedule meant she was always working late into the night. She was exhausted, and poor Gaga started suffering from anxiety when she was on the road.

LIFE ON THE ROAD

She spent a lot of nights working on new music on her tourbus, driving through Eastern Europe, and working through some dark times in her mind, which inspired the heavier sound of a lot of the songs. 'I wrote every piece on the road - no songs about money, no songs about fame. I wrote it for my fans, so I wrote everything in between' Gaga later explained.

'I WROTE ABOUT EVERYTHING I DIDN'T WRITE ON *THE FAME*. WHILE TRAVELLING THE WORLD FOR TWO YEARS, I'VE ENCOUNTERED SEVERAL MONSTERS, EACH REPRESENTED BY A DIFFERENT SONG ON THE NEW RECORD.'

FAMILY MATTERS

While she was on the road, she had one particular demon that she had to fight. She had always been really close to her dad, but he had been living with a serious heart condition for 15 years. Being a fighter, he didn't want to have surgery. Instead, he just wanted his life to take its natural course.

But everything changed when Gaga was away touring. He started to get worse, but Gaga couldn't leave the road because she had thousands of fans counting on her. 'My mom called me and I was very depressed. I was on tour and I couldn't leave, so I went into the studio and I wrote this song 'Speechless', and it's about these phone calls,' she says. 'My dad used to call me . . . and I wouldn't know what to say. I was speechless and I just feared that I would lose him and I wouldn't be there.'

Eventually Gaga persuaded her dad to go into hospital for the operation, which was a great success. She rushed to her dad's side while he was recovering.

Gaga's other inspiration in writing 'Speechless' was to remind her fans to treasure their parents. 'I say this with such sincerity; I wrote this song 'Speechless' that was this plea to my father. I sent it to him. I have a lot of fans who are really lovely, young, troubled fans, but I want to remind them that you only get one set of parents.'

RELEASING THE FAME MONSTER

Originally, Gaga's record company had wanted to re-release her debut album *The Fame* with an extra eight songs on it, the new songs she had been working on while on tour. But she knew the material she had written on tour was good enough to be released as a new album, but she had to persuade her record label to get them to agree. 'In the midst of my creative journey composing *The Fame Monster,* there came an exciting revelation that this was in fact my [second] album,' she said. 'I would not add, nor take away any songs from this EP. It is a complete conceptual and musical body of work that can stand on its own two feet. It doesn't need *The Fame.*'

The feisty New Yorker also had trouble persuading her labels about the new look she wanted to adopt for the album's design: darker and edgier. 'I had lots of arguments with my record labels about my album covers because they were sort of classic and simple,' she said. 'I am ready for the future, but I mourn the past. You have to let go of things. You have to mourn them like a death so that you can move on, and that's sort of what the album is about.'

> 'BRITNEY IS THE QUEEN OF POP.
> I WAS LEARNING FROM HER.'
> *Gaga on working with Britney*

GAGA, BEYONCE AND KANYE!

During the writing of *The Fame Monster*, Gaga had also made friends with two pop music icons – Beyoncé and Kanye West. Gaga met Beyoncé at an awards ceremony and the girls hit it off straight away – agreeing to collaborate on tracks that would feature on each of their forthcoming albums – 'Videophone' on Beyoncé's album, and 'Telephone' on Gaga's.

Gaga's project with Kanye West was much bigger than a track – together they planned a stage extravaganza that would change the world of pop music tours forever! *The Fame Kills Tour* was well into its planning stage and the pair had started rehearsing when disaster struck. At the MTV Video Music Awards, a very drunk Kanye barged his way onto the stage and interrupted Taylor Swift, who was giving an acceptance speech for having won Best Female Video. He grabbed the microphone from Taylor and protested that Beyoncé's video was much better! He was booed offstage, and disappeared from the public eye after the show. A few weeks later, *The Fame Kills Tour* was called off.

But rather than be disheartened, Gaga upped her game and announced to her fans that she would instead be launching a solo world tour, as she had been planning to do some months later anyway. Her fans were thrilled, and tickets sold out within hours of going on sale!

'I'M NO TV TALENT-SHOW WANNABE, I DID THIS THE WAY YOU'RE SUPPOSED TO: I WORKED HARD. I'M INVOLVED IN EVERY ASPECT OF MY WORK. I'M NOT LIKE SOME SINGERS, WHO JUST TURN UP TO PUT THEIR VOCALS OVER ANOTHER PERSON'S SONG.'
Gaga on her talent

The tour covered the US, Canada, the UK, New Zealand, Australia, Japan, Sweden, Germany and many more countries – even going to South America!

'It's still called *Monster Ball*, but it's more of a musical and less of a concert. It has a New York theme, it's a story, and the story is that me and my friends are in New York and we're going to the *Monster Ball*, and we get lost.'

The Monster Ball combined all the hits from *The Fame* with Gaga's new kick-ass material, like *Bad Romance, Dance in the Dark* and *Alejandro*. The show was even bigger and more extravagant than *The Fame Ball*, with new amazing costumes including the futuristic silver jewelled jumpsuit with lightbulbs on, the elaborate cream ecto-skeleton, a silver bodysuit, a black feathered jacket and a gold Egyptian-style crown and bodysuit. The performance ended with Gaga faking her death, and then a video of her getting a heart-shaped tattoo on her shoulder with the word 'Dad' in the middle of it. Aw!

'SHE IS SUCH A BEAUTIFUL PERSON. I HAD KIND OF LOST FAITH A LITTLE BIT IN MEETING ARTISTS IN THE BUSINESS - AND THEN I MET BEYONCÉ.'

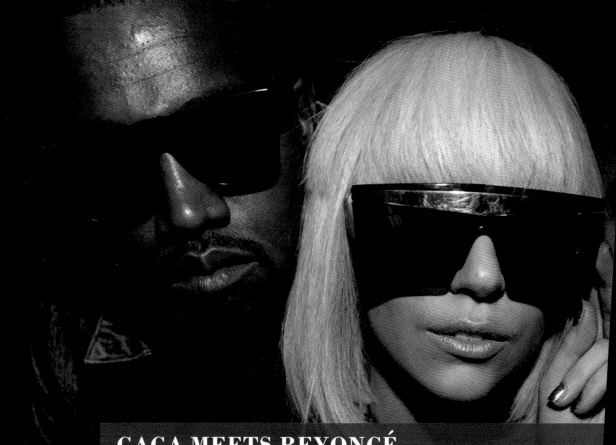

GAGA MEETS BEYONCÉ
Gaga's song *Telephone* was originally written for Britney's album Circus. But when it failed to make it onto the album, Gaga made the awesome decision to record it with Beyoncé for *The Fame Monster*!

DON'T CALL HER STEFANI!
'I don't appreciate when people call me Stefani, because if they don't know me, I feel like it's their way of acting like they do . . . they're completely ignoring my creative existence . . . Lady Gaga is who I am.'

WORKAHOLIC GAGA
'I don't go to nightclubs. You don't see pictures of me falling out of a club drunk. I don't go – and that's because I usually go and then, you know, a whiskey and a half into it –I got to get back to work.'

LOVE AND ROMANCE
♡

If there's one thing that this bubbly New York chick has had problems with all her life, it's guys! 'My problem area is definitely men,' she confides. 'I've only ever really been in love once. He didn't want me to do this job. He wanted me to stay at home, so I left. It broke my heart, but also made me realise music is my first love.'

After a relationship in her late teens broke her heart, Gaga has made sure that music is number one in her life and any boys have to play second best to that. 'My music's never going to roll over in bed one morning and tell me it doesn't love me anymore. I have a problem with rejection,' she says.

She did manage to find romance on the set of one of her videos though. She met the Los Angeles entrepreneur Speedy on the set of her music video for 'LoveGame', and although they were just friends at first, they soon became inseparable. The couple were spotted out and about by the paps everywhere – even in Hawaii, where they went to try and get some privacy!

But alas, it wasn't to be. A year of touring and hard work in the studio meant that the relationship wasn't going anywhere, so the couple broke up. Gaga was sad about it – but ultimately she knew she would always have her work to fall back on. 'You know, I probably won't ever settle down,' she said after the break up. 'Part of me would love all that, but the bigger part of me knows it's never going to happen. I don't think I'm cut out for love and marriage. Music and my art are the big things in my life. I know whatever happens they won't cheat on me and they'll never let me down. Men nearly always do.'

So for now, the busy singer is single – she'd rather devote her life to her art than any boyfriends.

'I DO LOVE BRITISH MEN, THOUGH. THEY'RE SMART AND THE ACCENT IS BORDERLINE PRETENTIOUS, WHICH I LOVE.'

'I DON'T NEED A MAN. I MIGHT SOMETIMES WANT A MAN, BUT I DON'T NEED ONE. I EARN MY MONEY, I CREATE MY ART, I KNOW WHERE I AM GOING.'

'I THINK MY PARENTS THOUGHT I'D BE MARRIED BY NOW, BUT I REBELLED AGAINST THAT WHOLE LIFE. I'M UNCONVENTIONAL, I'M A REBEL.'

'ON FIRST LISTEN, 'PAPARAZZI' MIGHT COME OFF AS A LOVE SONG TO CAMERAS, AND IN ALL HONESTY, ON ONE LEVEL IT IS ABOUT WOOING THE PAPARAZZI AND WANTING FAME. BUT, IT'S NOT TO BE TAKEN COMPLETELY SERIOUSLY. IT'S ABOUT EVERYONE'S OBSESSION WITH THAT IDEA. BUT, IT'S ALSO ABOUT WANTING A GUY TO LOVE YOU AND THE STRUGGLE OF WHETHER YOU CAN HAVE SUCCESS, OR LOVE, OR BOTH.'
Gaga on the hit song 'Paparazzi'

STYLE AND FASHION

Gaga has always had a very unique sense of fashion and style – even as a young teenager at school she was always experimenting with different looks. As she got older, she soon realised the way she wanted to look – and that was never ever to wear trousers!

It's almost impossible to list all the looks Gaga has been seen in, but the most memorable of them included a dress made of bubbles, a steel dress, and an outfit made entirely from Kermit the Frog!

'I'VE ALWAYS BEEN AN OUTSPOKEN AND EXTREME DRESSER.'

She's always been innovative when it comes to fashion, even before she made it big, and was living with no money in New York. She would buy cheap bras from bargain stores and customise them herself with stick-on mirror tiles and chains, creating mirror-ball bikini tops that she could wear onstage. Now her costumes are even bigger and more outrageous than she could ever have imagined!

Gaga's fashion icons are classic pop stars like Grace Jones and David Bowie. Her mum was really into classic designers, which is a love that Gaga inherited – so she's also really inspired by designers like Gabbana, Versace, Gucci, Chanel, but she also always tries to make everything look her own.

GAGA'S FASHION FAVOURITES
Make-up MAC COSMETICS. 'IT'S SO NEW YORK.'
Shades 'I LOVE MY VERSACE VINTAGE.'
Bag 'ANY BY YSL.'
Shoes 'RIGHT NOW, MY VINTAGE CHANEL BOOTS.'

THE
FUTURE
IS
BRIGHT!

QUEEN OF POP

When a singer has crammed as much into their young life as Lady Gaga has, it's almost impossible to know what on earth she'll do next!

She's risen from the streets of the Lower East Side in New York to become one of the most famous Ladies of Pop. She's sold more music downloads than any other artist and sold over 10 million albums worldwide!

THE SKY'S THE LIMIT

So what is next in the world of Gaga? There's a new album in the making and tours along with that, and also some collaborations in the works. There are still rumours that Gaga and Kanye will resurrect their *Fame Kills Tour* – and even rumours that she might end up working with Susan Boyle! 'I love Susan Boyle,' Gaga gushed. 'She is my woman of the year. She has achieved more in this year than most artists will in a lifetime. Our styles are different, but it would be great to work with somebody of that talent.'

She also wants to explore other avenues as well as music, and is planning to work with fashion designers and do performance pieces on a runway show. Wow!

Ultimately though, Gaga's main aim is to keep inspiring her little monsters, who keep her going through all her anxiety and self-doubt. We can't wait to see what she comes up with next!

'YOU CAN SAY THE PHILOSOPHY OF GAGA IS
FASHION-MUSIC-TECHNOLOGY-PERFORMANCE
ART.'

'I WAS BORN AND RAISED IN NEW YORK CITY. I AM
INSPIRED BY STREET FASHION AND THE ATTITUDE.
ANDY WARHOL IS A HUGE INSPIRATION OF MINE
AND I HAVE A LOT OF POP ART ELEMENTS IN THE
SHOW. I AM SO PASSIONATE ABOUT MY MUSIC.'

PICTURE CREDITS

All pictures and poster courtesy of Getty Images.

ACKNOWLEDGEMENTS

Posy Edwards would like to thank Jane Sturrock, James Martindale,
Helen Ewing, Nicola Crossley, Helia Phoenix, Hannah Lewis and Rich Carr

First published in hardback in Great Britain in 2010 by
Orion Books an imprint of the Orion Publishing Group Ltd
Orion House, 5 Upper St Martin's Lane, London WC2H 9EA

An Hachette Livre UK Company

1 3 5 7 9 10 8 6 4 2

A CIP catalogue record for this book is available from the British Library.

ISBN: 978 1 4091 2314 9

Designed by Smith & Gilmour, London
Printed in Spain by Cayfosa

www.orionbooks.co.uk